SAILING KNOTS

J. Altimiras

SAILING KNOTS

Translated by Tom Willis

Photographs by M. Casenelles

ARCO PUBLISHING, INC.
New York

Published by Arco Publishing, Inc.
215 Park Avenue South, New York, NY 10003
1984

Library of Congress Catalog Card Number: 84-70914
ISBN 0-668-06266-5

Printed in Spain by Grijelmo S.A.

Contents

Introduction

For centuries knot-tying was an art practised almost exclusively by seamen. Drivers, farmers, weavers and craftsmen might all have used ropes and lines in the course of their work, but to nothing like the same extent as those who earned their living from the sea.

The increasingly larger dimensions and more complex rigging plans of sailing ships demanded progressively more specialised techniques of ropework. Those sailors have left us a heritage consisting of a huge number of different knots for securing ropes. Most of them were designed to perform specific functions on board a ship.

The length of sailing ship voyages, often several months, led to the invention of a whole series of aesthetically pleasing knots developed by sailors spending their free time engaged in their own traditional crafts. Since then fancywork — the term for such creative ropework — has enjoyed the status of an accepted art.

Today the tall ships have almost disappeared and engine power has replaced the wind — though maybe not forever. Sail training vessels are continuing the traditions of the age of sail, and the phenomenal growth in sport and leisure boating has brought thousands of new converts to this ancient craft.

The skill used to be learned during an arduous apprenticeship and deepened in the course of a lifetime spent at sea. But nowadays what used to take years to master can be acquired from clearly written and richly illustrated books in hours.

And that is the purpose of this book: to describe, as clearly and in as much detail as possible, just something of what can be done with ropes on board a boat — in other words, to give an insight into the art of knot-tying.

There are many people who regard it as pointless to waste their valuable time on such tasks. This may be because the skippers of modern pleasure boats, with their plastic hulls, aluminium masts and stainless steel standing rigging feel no need to learn such elementary concepts as the correct way to secure ropes. In the age of autopilots, satellite navigation systems and Doppler-effect logs, a knot like the bowline seems archaic and to serve no purpose. Nothing could be further from the truth, of course. Ropework has continued to evolve, has adapted to modern needs, and familiarity with the knot is still necessary for the handling of any boat, sail or power.

In this book you will learn the modern art of handling synthetic rope and braided rope, which cannot be spliced like conventional three-strand twisted ropes. You will also learn to carry out tasks on board that will save time and money, quite apart from the satisfaction that will come with doing a job well.

It may be these first tasks on board — such as splicing a rope tail into a wire genoa halyard, or making an eye splice in a mooring warp — that will stimulate a greater interest in working with rope and wire leading you to discover for yourself the fascination of fancywork. As well as learning an attractive new hobby, it will enable you to give your boat the personal touch that a production-line model lacks.

The further you go, the more satisfyingly creative ropework becomes. Whether you're making a deck mat or a Turk's Head on a stanchion, or putting a monkey's fist in a heaving line, you will be spending your time making something attractive, something perfect and in so doing you will find some relief from the stress of modern life.

There is no better way of finding contentment than to spend an evening happily involved in making an eye splice or a long splice — and making it so well that it becomes a pleasure to use. First you must get to grips with the basics, the simplest and most common knots and hitches.

In this book we cover 50 different examples of knots, splices and fancywork, beginning with the simplest, such as the overhand knot and the half hitch, and moving on to the complex ones such as an eye splice in wire or short splice. We have kept the number of knots down so as to be able to give each the description it needs and in order to devote the space to better and clearer illustrations.

It's a fact that learning knots and mastering ropework will help you sharpen the intellect. Both should be taught at the earliest possible age. With all knots there is not a very obvious connection between theory and practice. The first knots you learn simply by practice and constant repetition; but then — like when you learn to read — you begin to understand the theory behind ropework. From this point on you become amazed by the ingenuity of the inventor of a knot. In the end the moment comes when the knot becomes an intellectual exercise, either to provide an answer in an emergency or to give you scope for a little creativity.

The art of the knot-tyer belongs to the cultural heritage of every sailor, but it's not limited to those who go boating. Other sports, like climbing or fishing, and many handicrafts, demand a good knowledge and understanding of ropework. For this reason, although it's aimed chiefly at the sailing fraternity, this book should prove useful for many people.

You should continually practise this ropework if you want to derive maximum benefit from the lessons in this book. Practice is essential, for both the simple and the complex jobs. You have to go on and on doing each task until it becomes second nature. Practise on board whenever you have the chance.

For some jobs, such as an eye splice in wire or palm-and-needle whippings, a tool will be necessary. The most important are described in the following section. There are many good sailors who know their knots, but don't necessarily know when to use each. For this reason we have split them into different groups:

- Knots in a single line
- Knots using two lines
- Whippings and stopper knots
- Rope and wirework, and fancywork

In each classification the tasks are given in order of increasing difficulty.

Tools

As we have already said, there are a number of tools available that make working with rope and wire considerably easier. Let us take a look at a few.

Net needle

A net needle is usually made of wood, but can also be found in plastic versions. It is used for making nets and in fancywork. A line is wound on to the centre of the needle, which is then threaded through the mesh to make the net, unrolling the required amount of line as you go. This avoids the need to pull the full length of line through the net at every weave.

Sailmaker's needle

This is a strong, three-sided needle used for repairing sails, and can be found in any good chandlery. As with household needles there are various sizes or numbers graded according to the thread used. In addition to its value in mending sailcloth or dodgers, the sailmaker's needle is also used extensively in ropework, especially whipping and seizing. It is therefore worth keeping several different sizes in the bosun's locker.

Fid and pusher

Fairly recent additions to the yacht inventory, this pair of tools will be needed if you want to splice braid-on-braid ropes. They are graded according to the rope size and strength.

Fid

These wooden spikes, called fids, are used to splice twisted rope. They are made from particularly hard wood, tapering sharply to a fine point. Spikes made of steel (marlin spikes) are used for splicing wire, which is easier if the spike is oval in cross section and flattened towards the tip.

It goes without saying that sharp spikes can cause serious injuries. Beware.

Swedish fid

These are metal spikes formed with a hollowed-out centre for feeding strands into the interior of lines. Whether they were invented by the Scandinavians or not is uncertain.

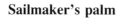

Sailmaker's palm

The palm is a strip of leather that fits over the palm of your hand, with a hole for the thumb. In the middle is a metal plate indented like a thimble against which the head of the needle is held so that you can force the needle through heavy-duty canvas or rope.

Working with a palm takes a little practice. Incidentally, there are right- and left-hand models available.

Shears

You should carry on board two pairs of best quality stainless steel shears: a small pair of scissors for cutting light line, and a full-sized pair of heavy-duty shears for other jobs. A word of warning — don't let them fall into the hands of either the cook or the children.

Thimbles

These are available in brass, galvanised iron, stainless steel or plastic. Used to protect the rope or wire in an eye splice from chafe, they are made to specific breaking strengths to match the strength of the rope or wire. As with shackles, you will need a good selection of various sizes.

Wooden mallet

A medium-sized mallet is very useful for working a splice into shape. It will also come in handy when pressing a thimble into sailcloth or inserting a spike into hard-laid wire.

Shackles

Usually in brass or stainless steel, shackles are used to join together two sections of rigging. A wide variety of different sizes and types is indispensable.

Sailor's knife

Ideally you should have two or three knives on board. One should be used only for working with wire, so that it can be kept sharp; it should be very strong, with a blade of top-quality stainless steel. Like the spike, a sharp knife can cause serious injury if mishandled, and it should therefore be stowed in a special place known only to the people who are likely to need it.

Glossary

Bend By definition, a knot used to join two lines, e.g. sheetbend; but the fisherman's bend and several other so-called bends are exceptions to this rule.

Bight General name for an open curve in the line of a rope. If it is closed it becomes a loop.

Bitts A single fitting consisting of a pair of mooring bollards.

Boltrope Rope sewn into the luff and foot of a mainsail or the luff of a foresail.

Breaking strength A rope's tensile strength — the load under which it will break. Maximum working loads are always much lower.

Cleat A deck fitting used to temporarily make lines fast to.

Deck eye Similar to the above, but can also be used to alter the lead or direction of a line.

Elasticity The capacity of a rope to return to its original shape after being stretched. Any rope loses its elasticity at loads greatly below its breaking strength.

Fancywork Creative ropework, usually more decorative than functional.

Free end (also called **working part**) The part of a rope furthest from the part under load.

Guardrails Horizontal wire safety rails on the edge of the deck.

Hitch A knot used to tie a line to a spar or fitting. As with the term bend, there are exceptions.

Kink In wire, a small eye caused by a twist in the line. A kink should always be cleared by untwisting before any load is put on the wire.

Knot Catch-all term with no precise definition — other than that bends and hitches are both knots, but splices aren't.

Lay The twist in a rope (as in right-hand lay).

Rope A word almost never used by sailors; virtually all types of rope have names of their own that define their form or function precisely, such as hawser, warp, halyard, etc.

Round turn A 360° turn taken by a rope around a spar. A 180° turn where the rope ends up pointing in the direction from which it came, is a half-turn.

Running rigging Rope or wire used to control the sails.

Score The groove between neighbouring strands of a twisted rope.

Seizing A method of binding together two ropes using thinner line.

Serving Similar to whipping, but used to cover a completed splice with marline or other thick twine.

Sheave The pulley wheel in a block. Halyard sheaves are often fitted directly into the mast.

Splice A method of joining a rope to itself or to another rope by interweaving the separate strands. Can also be used for wire cable.

Stanchion Vertical post supporting the guardrails.

Standing part The part of a rope that comes under load.

Standing rigging Rope or wire, more or less fixed in position, supporting the mast.

Strand Three-strand rope is known as hawser-laid four-strand as shroud-laid. The strands are made up of yarns twisted in the opposite direction to the lay of the rope.

Tackle Set of blocks used to reduce the effort required to haul in a line under strain.

Terminal A fitting used to connect the end of a wire cable to another fitting.

Thimble A teardrop-shaped metal or plastic eye used to shape an eye splice and prevent chafe.

Twine Thin line of various types for various uses, as in sail twine, whipping twine, etc.

Warp Rope used for mooring or anchoring (in the latter case also known as an anchor rode).

Whipping A method of preventing the end of a rope from unravelling by wrapping it tightly with twine.

Yarn Bundles of fibres are twisted to form yarns, which are then twisted again to form the strands of a rope.

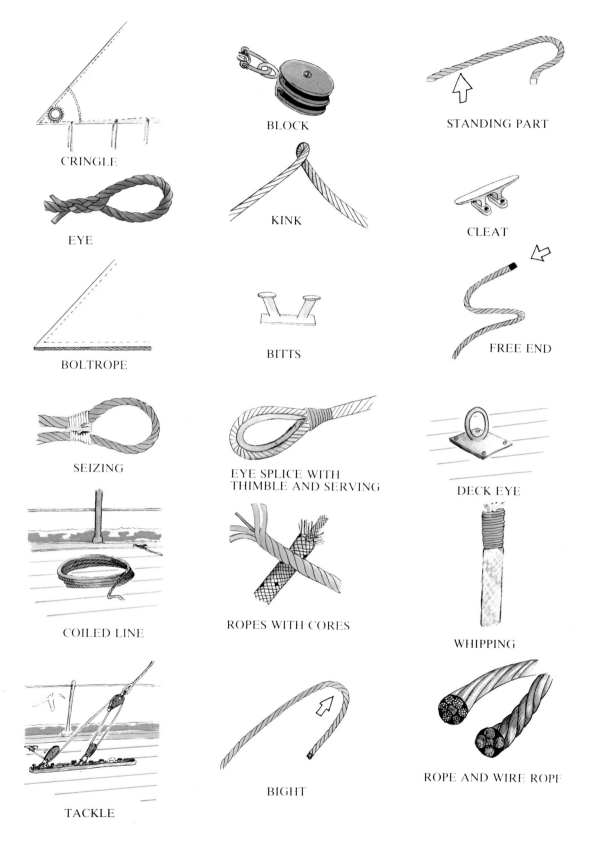

CRINGLE

BLOCK

STANDING PART

EYE

KINK

CLEAT

BOLTROPE

BITTS

FREE END

SEIZING

EYE SPLICE WITH
THIMBLE AND SERVING

DECK EYE

COILED LINE

ROPES WITH CORES

WHIPPING

TACKLE

BIGHT

ROPE AND WIRE ROPE

13

Ropes

Rope can be defined in a variety of different ways: by material — natural or artificial fibre; by its manufacture — twisted or braided; by size — circumference or diameter, or terms denoting size, from cable and hawser down to twine.

There are two types of rigging to be found on board a boat. Standing rigging includes ropes and, more often, wires that are more or less fixed in position, such as the shrouds and stays; running rigging, as the name implies, includes sheets, halyards, downhauls, running backstays and so on. Most standing rigging today is made of stainless steel, while running rigging is usually a mixture of wire and artificial-fibre rope. Sheets are often made of natural fibre, which gives a better grip.

Natural fibre rope

At one time all rope was made of natural fibre: hemp, manila, jute, sisal, cotton or coir. Manila is the name given to the fibre taken from a banana plant native to the Philippines, which produces fibres over six foot long; in addition, it floats and is very durable.

Hemp rope does not float. When it is used it is sometimes tarred to prevent rot.

Cotton, soft and with good gripping properties, is in common use for sheets, and is also used as the core for lines with an artificial-fibre outer sheath. Rope made of jute is practically unavailable nowadays. Sisal fibres are shorter and rougher than hemp, and rope made of this material is coarse and feels hard.

Coir rope, made from coconut fibre, floats and has a fairly high resistance to rot, but a low breaking strain.

With the exception of cotton, natural-fibre ropes are never ̲ed on the average yacht.

To make a rope the fibres are first checked for length, with ̲ose that are not long enough discarded or used for filling ̲attresses, furniture and so on. The selected fibres are then ̲eaned, combed and cut to a uniform length of ̲pproximately 24 in (60 cm) before being twisted into yarns. ̲he yarns are twisted in the opposite direction to make each ̲trand, the strands (three or sometimes four) are then twisted

Fibres

Yarns

Strands

Rope

The fibres are twisted together to form yarns, which are then twisted in the opposite direction to make the strands. Usually three strands are then twisted together to give the finished line.

in the same direction as the original fibres to make the finished rope. Most ropes are right-hand laid, which means that the strands travel up the rope towards the right, like a corkscrew. If the rope consists of three strands, it is termed 'hawser-laid'; four strands, 'shroud-laid'. Very thick ropes, called hawsers, are not used on board pleasure boats, but there is an abundance of very thin line that is available: seizing and whipping twine, sailmaker's twine and a variety of two- and three-strand twisted line of high quality.

Natural fibre rope has the major disadvantage that it doesn't like getting wet. The fibres take up water and swell, so that the outer ones stretch badly. This will also affect the rope's cohesive strength, and both these aspects together will result in substantial reduction of the rope's breaking strength.

Some fibres, like manila, do not stand up well to damp, while others, such as coir, are more resistant. Nevertheless, no natural fibre should ever be stowed away while still wet. It should always be put away not only quite dry, but also without any kinks.

Finally, it is important to make certain that a natural fibre rope is never overloaded. If the rope ever reaches, or almost reaches its breaking point, throw it away. It will probably have structurally altered to the point where even a relatively low load would cause it to give way.

Artificial fibre rope

Within the space of a few short years artificial fibre ropes have almost totally replaced natural fibre, thanks to their higher strength and rot resistance, their uniformity and the fact that they are much easier to manufacture.

Virtually all artificial fibre ropes are made of polyester (Dacron), polyamide (nylon) or polyethylene (polypropylene). The best material for general use is nylon; it wears well, has a long life, doesn't rot and will not float. It is also very elastic. This latter characteristic makes it especially suitable for anchor and mooring warps, less so for halyards. Finally, nylon ropes are comfortable to hold and use. There are available low-elasticity grades, usually achieved through a braided outer sheath or by loading the rope to within a few pounds of its breaking strain, a process called pre-stretching.

Polypropylene is not as refined as nylon, but it does possess an occasionally useful advantage: it floats. Polyester, used to make sailcloth under the trade name of Dacron, grips well and is therefore valuable as a material for the outer sheath of braided rope. In another form it is known as Terylene. Polypropylene ropes are hard on the hands, sometimes fail to grip under load, but are light in weight and have their uses.

Artificial fibre rope is made in a number of different ways. It can be laid up like natural fibre rope, in other words twisted into yarns, then strands, then line of any diameter; or it can be formed into a braided rope with an outer sheath around a central core. As the fibres of an artificial fibre rope can be made as long as you like, the eventual line is much more uniform than natural fibre equivalents, whose fibres vary enormously in strength and length and can therefore produce weak spots in the rope.

Artificial fibres can also be dyed during manufacture, so that the running rigging of a boat can be colour-coded for easier recognition.

A significant problem associated with artificial fibre ropes is that they do not stand up well to heat. Friction can raise the local temperature of a part of the line considerably, with the result that the rope wears a great deal more than a natural fibre rope would. This disadvantage also gives synthetic ropes an advantage of sorts in that the fibres at the end of the rope can be heat-welded together, doing away with the need for a conventional whipping. Ropes should therefore be cut using either an electric hot-wire cutter or a knife heated over the cooker flame.

Artificial fibre ropes can be damaged by oil and grease, which will reduce their breaking strength although at the

A twisted rope can be made of three or four strands. A four-strand (shroud-laid) line will have a central core.

same time friction damage will be reduced. Perhaps future nylon ropes will have some silicon added to reduce the effects of friction-induced high temperatures.

Regular cleaning of synthetic ropes will help to keep friction damage to a minimum, but another effective method is to sheathe your lines in plastic tubing at points where friction is likely.

Artificial fibre ropes can be cleaned in lukewarm water and detergent. It is recommended that you dry the rope before restowing it to prevent mildew; although it won't harm the fibres, this is unsightly. Synthetic fibres are affected by ultraviolet radiation, however; ropes that are not in current

Another type of rope consists of an outer braided sheath around an inner core.

use should be stowed below deck to reduce exposure to the sun and thereby prolong their life.

Wire rope

A large proportion of the rigging of a yacht is made up of wire rope. Not only is it much stronger than natural fibre rope of an equivalent weight, it is by comparison totally inelastic. Since it doesn't stretch, wire is frequently used to make shrouds and stays to support the mast, and guardrails for the safety of the crew. On bigger craft, wire can also be found in the form of halyards, as part of the running rigging.

Galvanised steel wire rope

This consists of separate strands of steel wire, galvanised to prevent corrosion before being laid up in the form of a rope. Unfortunately, galvanisation on its own is not enough to cope with the effects of the wet, salt-laden marine environment, and so this type of wire should ideally be greased or painted with several coats of paint every six months.

That having been said, galvanised wire is very dependable, never failing without giving due notice. Another advantage lies in its relative cheapness. The separate strands are also flexible enough to make splicing fairly easy.

Most wire rope is made up round a core of hemp of sisal. This may constitute the centre of the cable itself, with the strands twisted round it, or the centre of each strand, which gives the whole greater flexibility and makes it more suitable for running rigging applications. Halyards must be kept well greased to prevent internal friction and prolong their life.

If the wire has a single rope core, the same rules apply as for natural fibre rope; i.e., try to prevent the core becoming and remaining wet. This can be done, as has been said, by painting or greasing.

It is vitally important to ensure that a wire cable with a kink

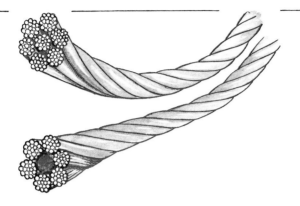

Wire rope is made by twisting together strands consisting of separate bunches of wire filament. The picture shows two types, both made up of six strands, with one twisted round a rope core, the other round a core formed by a seventh strand.

in it is not subjected to load. If it is, the kink will become permanent, and the mechanical strength of the cable will be substantially reduced. To remove a kink, lay the wire flat and beat it with a wooden mallet in the area of the deformation.

Wire rope should be coiled in the form of a figure 8, with reasonably large loops.

Inspect your wire rigging from time to time, as it does not have an unlimited lifespan. Broken strands are a clear indication that it it time to renew the cable, quite apart from the fact that loose wires can easily gash your hands or tear your sails.

Stainless steel wire

Most yachtsmen cannot spend an unlimited amount of time on their boat. They therefore need materials that require a minimum of maintenance, such as glassfibre for the hull and stainless steel for the rigging.

Ninety-nine per cent of yachts are equipped with stainless steel standing rigging, and in many cases halyards, guardrails and other parts of the running rigging are made of the same material.

Stainless steel is considerably more expensive than

galvanised, but this does not necessarily mean that it is stronger in every case.

Stainless is available in several different grades depending on the quantity of molybdenum and other metals used in its manufacture.

Some of these grades are unsurpassed for marine use. The most common choices are Type 302/304 (in the USA) and Type 316 (Europe). The former has a higher breaking strain, the latter a greater resistance to oxidation.

For standing rigging wire is generally made up in the pattern 1 x 19. This consists of nineteen separate strands slightly larger in diameter than the strands used in galvanised steel cable. An advantage of this form lies in its limited elasticity, which means that shrouds and stays maintain their tension. On racing boats the stays will often be in the form of rod rigging, which can be adjusted at the terminals to get the correct tension and then left. Neither 1 x 19 nor rod rigging can be spliced, which adds to the cost since the ends must be fitted with special terminals such as the Norseman or Nicro types.

Running rigging and guardrails demand wire rope with several strands each made up of a number of filaments, with or without a core. Although this type of wire can be expected to stretch, it will flex more, which makes it easier to use and splice (though not as easy as galvanised steel wire).

Stainless steel wire requires very little maintenance, but you should bear in mind that wear is going to be greater at the terminals. It is therefore advisable to oil these parts and then give them a further protective coating of thick grease or silicon. Spots of electrolytic corrosion should also be cleaned off with a wire brush and then rubbed well with a soft cloth and metal polish.

Terminals

Wire, unlike rope, cannot be tied into knots, and some types cannot be spliced. At each end of a wire cable, therefore, you need to fit a terminal so that the wire can be attached to rigging screws, eyebolts and so on.

One way of fixing a terminal to wire is to form it into an eye around a thimble and fit U-bolt clamps, ideally three, at intervals along the standing part so that it grips the free end. These should be tightened progressively so that the last clamp (the one furthest from the thimble) is given the greatest torque.

This method is simple, but adequately secure for use as an emergency repair. The thimbles chosen should be of the largest available diameter, so that the wire is not overstressed at the eye.

Some forms of wire can be spliced around a thimble or joined together with a swaged terminal.

Stainless steel 1 x 19 is unsuitable for splicing, as the strands are too many and too unyielding, so a terminal of the Norseman type is generally used.

All these methods are within the scope of the boat owner and can be effected with the tools carried on board.

Swaged fittings are the most widely used of all, but require a special machine only found in boatyards or rigging lofts. They are very reliable, but have a major drawback; you cannot see whether the end is deteriorating, and since the wire will break when it does break at the end, you will not necessarily know when it is time to replace the cable. It is therefore important to keep the terminals well greased, especially at the point where the wire exits from the tube.

Knots and hitches

The following knots, hitches, seizings, whippings and splices are those that a sailor might need to know, but they may also be needed by anglers and climbers.

It should be obvious after the first few pages that most of the knots have several attributes in common. Most are quick and easy to make, and we have shown the easiest method in each case.

Some of them are simple to undo, even when under load. All of them are reliable and durable, and well suited to the purpose indicated. Finally, they are for the most part attractive to look at.

All these aspects are the attributes of a good knot. Easy to make and release, strong and attractive. As you read the book you will find yourself developing the familiarity and dexterity that is necessary in order to be able to give your ropework that professional touch. The speed with which you can make fast depends largely on how rapidly the man on the foredeck can tie a knot.

We have left out the Gordian knot, together with all those overhand half-knots that are ugly, difficult to undo and unreliable in use.

So that you know how difficult a particular knot is to execute, the descriptions are followed at the foot of each page by a symbol denoting the level of competence required. The symbols are:

Simple knots without problems

Knots that are slightly more difficult

Difficult knots, or those requiring some concentration and time

Overhand knot

This, the best known and simplest of all knots, is termed the overhand knot by sailors. It is never used on its own — in other words, only used with the eye shown in the lower picture around a spar or a ring — because otherwise it becomes difficult or impossible to release, especially when the line is wet.

It shouldn't really be used even to prevent the free end of a rope from fraying, where the figure of eight knot will do the job just as well without jamming.

If an unused line develops an overhand knot, undo it immediately before it's too late.

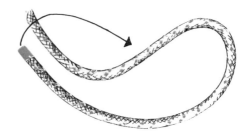

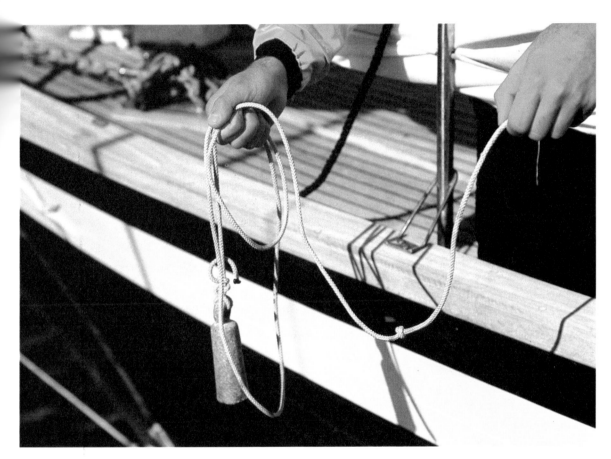

One possible function for the overhand knot is to mark a leadline; a knot at five fathoms, two at ten fathoms and so on, as shown in this picture. This isn't particularly seamanlike, though; the correct method is to mark the line with coloured tape or fabric.

Half hitch

The half hitch is a knot whose standing part
and free end lead off in the same direction.

On its own the half hitch will not hold. It
needs to be secured with a seizing, or a
second half hitch.

It is a simple knot, very easy to learn and
the basis of several other knots. To make
fast, say, to a ring, you would take a turn
round the ring and then finish off with two
half hitches.

To make the knot, lay the free end over
the standing part so that it forms an eye; then
take the end, pass it under the standing part
into the eye and then out again. Finish off
with a seizing or a second half hitch so that it
doesn't come undone.

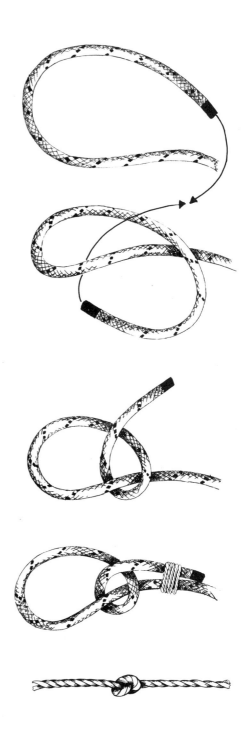

The half hitch is a knot so simple that beginners often use it to secure a line. Many people will use it in place of a clove hitch or bowline. If you lead the end through a fitting or round a stake twice and run two half hitches on top of it, the knot becomes firm enough, but might be difficult to release. The half hitch is therefore only really used to secure things fairly permanently, although it is frequently of value in securing the end of another knot.

You will often see the half hitch used in front of a seizing to reduce the load on the seizing itself.

Figure of eight

The overhand knot is well known to
landlubbers. But its place at sea is generally
taken by the figure of eight, so called because
it is shaped exactly like an 8.

Form an eye and lead the free end around
the back of the standing part, then through
the eye.

It isn't necessary to pull the figure of eight
tight, but you should ensure that there is
enough of a tail for you to grasp when the
knot is jammed up against a fairlead or
block.

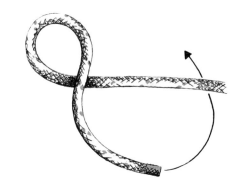

The figure of eight performs an important function on board, preventing the ends of running rigging from being pulled through blocks, rings or fairleads. It is used to finish off all sheets with the exception of spinnaker sheets, which in certain situations may have to be let fly immediately and without fuss. A further advantage over the overhand knot is that it can be released quickly even after it has been subjected to load. It is also bulkier. You can save yourself a lot of trouble if you make a habit of putting a figure of eight on all rope ends that cannot be allowed to slip through a fitting.

Slippery hitch

A variation on the half hitch, the slippery
hitch can be released instantly with a tug on
the free end, which makes it ideal as a knot
with which to secure a tow. Properly made, it
is very secure, although not very suitable as a
long-term solution since it can release itself if
the tension is not kept up in the standing
part.

To make the hitch, take a turn around the
mast, samson post or whatever the line is to
be secured to, lead the free end over the
standing part and double it up in the form of
a loop which you then feed under the
standing part and into the turn around the
mast. Pull the standing part tight, so that the
loop is gripped by the line round the mast.

Under the load the knot holds as firm as a
vice, but as soon as you no longer need it you
can simply release the hitch with a tug on the
free end.

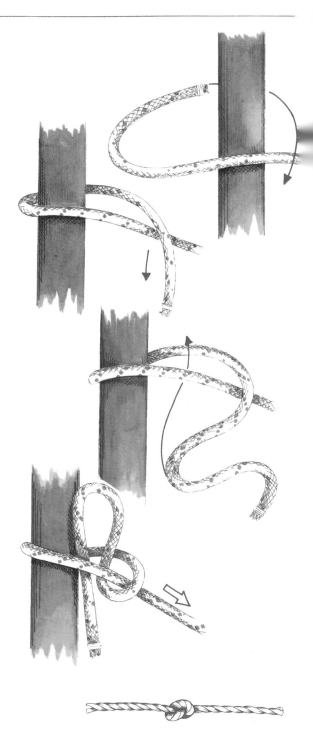

The slippery hitch is eminently suitable as a means of securing a tow line, as it is vital that these should be capable of immediate release in an emergency. Once the towed boat has been brought to its destination you need only to pull on the end to clear the tow line.

You can also use the hitch to secure the halyard to a guardrail, where it can be released in an instant, even from some distance away; provided that the tail is long enough, the knot can be cleared without even leaving the cockpit.

Clove hitch

The clove hitch is very easy to make, and is used extensively on most yachts. It is a knot that holds firmly, although it is not one hundred per cent secure. For this reason it is worth securing the free end separately, with a further half hitch or seizing round the standing part.

To make it you take a turn around the fitting to which you intend to secure the line, with the standing part on top of the fitting. Continuing in the same direction, take a further turn around, crossing over the first turn. The free end should be fed through the eye of the second turn. The standing part and the free end should still be pointing in the opposite directions.

To secure the hitch, pull from both sides. The free end should not be made too short, as it could then slip back through the knot.

The clove hitch can also be made in the hand, by forming two eyes and putting the eye in the standing part on top of the one further along. This is particularly useful when you want to make a knot in the middle of a line such as a burgee halyard.

The clove hitch will not hold when used in heavy-duty hawsers, made of synthetic materials.

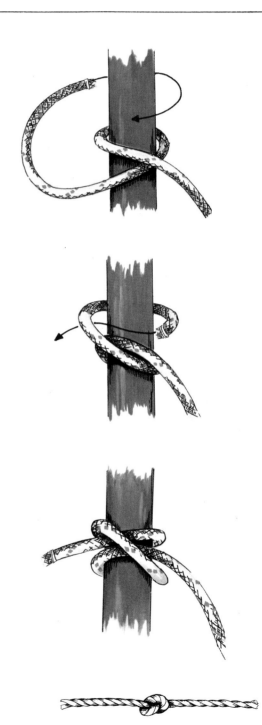

This hitch must be learnt and mastered on board, as it is quick to make, secure and grips more tightly the more load is placed upon it, without being difficult to release.

It is often used when making fast to a post or bollard, to secure fenders to guardrails or to tie up loose coiled warps to prevent them tangling.

Rolling hitch

The rolling hitch is derived from the clove hitch, but is significantly more secure. There is no need, as there is with the clove hitch, to finish the knot off with a half hitch or two to prevent slip. The rolling hitch is an impressive knot, reliable, easy to make and to undo. It grips itself, but only in one direction (see pages 80-81).

Take a turn round the spar with the rope, in such a way that the free end crosses over the standing part, then take another turn parallel and adjacent to the first, again so that the free end crosses over the standing part. Lead the free end round the spar again, but this time on the opposite side of the standing part to the two previous round turns, and finish off by tucking the end under the second round turn.

The knot will now hold in the direction of the standing part; in other words, if you pull downwards in the example shown in the picture.

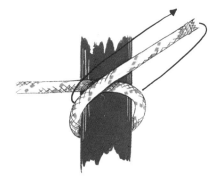

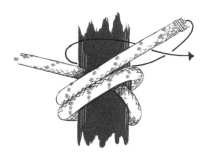

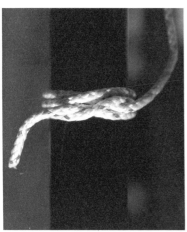

The rolling hitch is found on every sailboard nowadays securing the wishbone boom to the mast, a job it will perform better than any other knot.

You can also use it to make a line fast to a spar, a boom or other cylindrical-shaped object, on which any other form of knot could be expectd to slip.

Bowline

Probably the knot most widely used by
sailors and mountaineers alike, the bowline
possesses all the attributes of a good knot:
absolutely secure, easy to make and easy to
release, even when it has been subjected to
great strain.

To make a bowline, form an eye in the end
of the line far enough away from the rope
end to give you the size of loop you require.
In the eye the standing part should be
underneath.

Lead the free end underneath and through
the eye. Then take a turn round the standing
part and push the end back through the eye
again. Tighten the knot by holding the
standing part in one hand, the free end in the
other and pulling.

You now have a loop that cannot collapse
and will serve countless functions.

Sometimes you may want the free end to
end up on the outside of the big loop. To do
this, after you have led the end through the
eye as shown in the first drawing, take it
round the standing part in the opposite
directions to that shown in the middle
drawing (i.e. from left to right round the
back of the standing part).

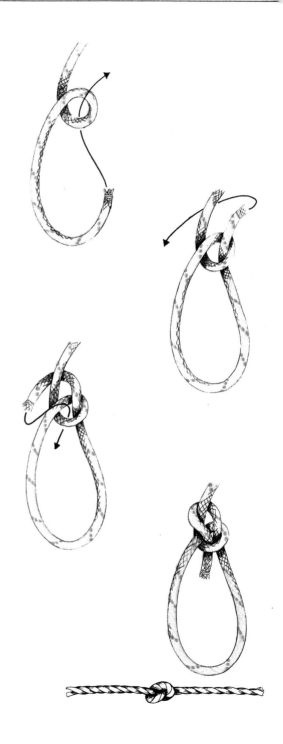

The bowline is one of the most commonly used knots. There are countless tasks it can perform on board, and it's likely that many sailors know only this knot. At any rate it is the one knot, above all others, that every crew member should know. You can use it to make fast to a bollard or a mooring ring. The bowline is extremely secure, even in polypropylene ropes, which are stiff and unyielding and which allow many knots to slip. The only point to be wary of is that the rope end is at least a hand's breadth from the eye so that it can't slip back through.

Bowline on the bight

This knot can be made anywhere in the middle of a line. Double the line, then make a loop of the required size. Form an eye as usual in the standing part, and pass the end through the eye from underneath upwards. Now open up the end, pull it forward and round the big loop so that it ends up encircling the standing part. Finally rearrange the two big loops so formed so that they are the same length and parallel. Then pull the knot tight.

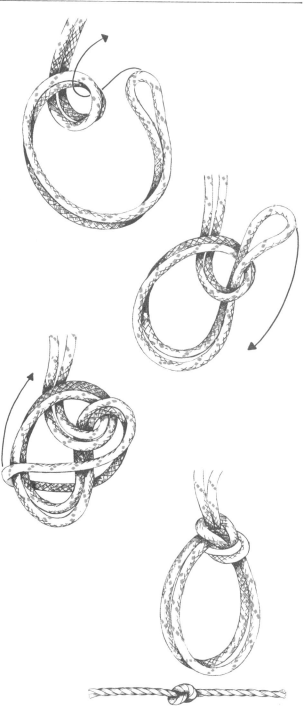

This double bowline is always useful when you need a bowline but don't have a convenient end. If you look at the photograph you will see that both ends of the line can be made fast separately and a bowline fixed in the middle. This may prove useful when, for instance, you want to put out a spring; in which case lead a line loosely from bow to stern, then get a crew member to leap ashore with the centre of the line and make fast using a double bowline to a bollard or cleat.

The bowline on the bight also comes in useful when you have to work overside. For climbing the mast you can use the bosun's chair, shown on the next page.

Bosun's chair

The bosun's chair is similar to the bowline on a bight in having two loops, but in this case they are adjustable.

Make two small eyes in the line with the part furthest from the free end underneath in each case. Then lead the free end through the eye from underneath so that it forms a large loop. Repeat the operation to get two loops of the same size. Now lead the end through the first eye, just as you would with a normal bowline — in other words through the eye, round the standing part and back into the eye.

There are variations of this knot with three or more big loops.

This knot is normally used to form a seat that can be used to hold a man secure while climbing the mast. One of the loops serves as a seat, the other as a backrest. With three loops two can be used for the seat, which is much more comfortable as the rope doesn't tend to cut into the thighs so much.

You can also always use a bosun's chair knot to make several loops in one end of a line, but take care — as one tightens, the other will loosen correspondingly.

Running bowline

This is the best knot to adopt when you want
one that is absolutely secure but has a loop of
variable diameter. It is derived from the
bowline, but the standing part remains within
the loop as shown in the lower of the two
illustrations. There are many uses for this slip
knot. The Spanish name *Ahorcaperros*
indicates one — used on a lead, it performs
the function of a choke chain for the training
of a headstrong dog.

To make it, form a big loop and lead the
free end around the standing part and back.
Then make a second, smaller eye in this loop,
lead the free end from underneath through
the eye and continue as for the normal
bowline.

Finally pull the bowline tight and adjust
the loop to the size you require.

A significantly easier method of making
this knot can be used in many cases: simply
form a conventional bowline and then push
the standing part down through the loop.

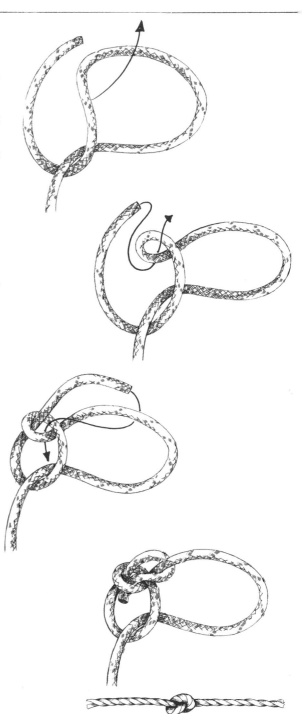

The running bowline can be used on board to pull a line tight. Often it proves useful in securing items of deck gear such as the life-raft, a tender or sailboard. It can also be used in towing and in cases where you need a knot that has to tighten up as the load increases. It is the most secure knot for a lasso.

Fisherman's bend

The fisherman's bend is a specialist knot used to make a line fast to a ring or spar. It has the major advantage of being easy to undo, even when the rope has become wet or been strained, as is the case with warps or anchor warps.

Take two turns round the ring with the line, then bring the free end back in front of the standing part and through the turns. Pull taut, make a half hitch around the standing part above the round turns and pull the half hitch taut. A more secure way of finishing off is to seize the tail to the standing part above the half hitch.

The small picture shows the ring of an anchor, from which the knot derives its alternative name of anchor bend. You will also notice that the knot has been secured with a seizing, an essential precaution against the rope working itself loose over the course of time and losing the anchor. Even two half hitches are not totally secure.

The fisherman's bend is sometimes used to attach fender lanyards to grabrails or stanchions, with at least one extra half hitch added for the sake of security.

Blackwall hitch

An exceptionally easy knot, the Blackwall hitch is used to make a line fast to a hook, for instance the hook of a crane in the marina.

Take a turn round the shank of the hook and lead the tail of the rope under the standing part. As soon as the load comes on, the standing part (shown arrowed in the top picture) will grip the free end firmly.

You can make one or two turns, and use either or both sides of the hook, but don't use smooth synthetic ropes, which may slip. The simplest version is that shown in the middle picture (called a Midshipman's hitch); the most secure is shown below with two turns round the inside of the hook (the double Blackwall).

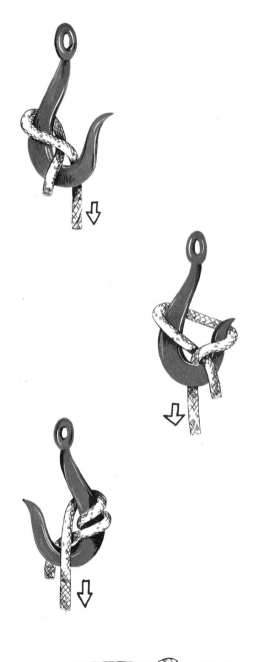

The Blackwall is the fastest and simplest way to secure a rope to a hook. Apart from that, there's little one can say about this hitch. It is not a hundred per cent secure, as it will slip as soon as the strain comes off; only the load causes it to grip.

When you have tied the hitch, hold on to the standing part until it comes under load, and watch out when the load eases. It is also important that both hook and line are of roughly the same diameter and are not too smooth-faced; natural fibre rope is the best.

Cleating a line

Lines are made fast to cleats using a hitch whose standing part grips the free end. It is simple to make, but also easy to make incorrectly. Every member of the crew should learn the right way to do it; the important thing is that the last turn should lead in the same direction as the standing part.

Take a turn round the base of the cleat, then bring the line over the front face of the cleat, below each of the horns in turn in a figure of eight pattern, and back underneath the crossing turn as shown in the bottom drawing. Pull tight.

A variation on this hitch demands a 360° turn round the base before beginning the crossing turns. In neither case is it necessary to make more than one and a half figures of eight before securing the hitch; it can be relied upon to hold itself firmly.

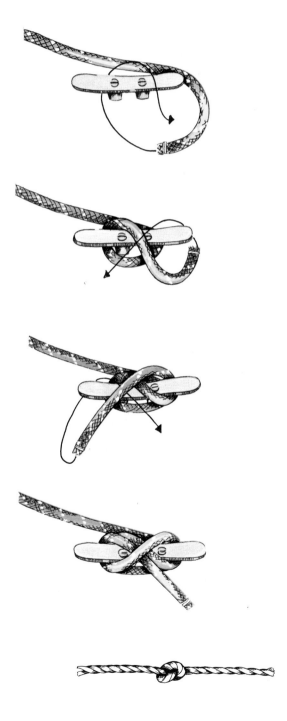

Cleats offer the most reliable method of securing any part of the running rigging that is going to have to be alternately made fast and released as a matter of course. The beginner will probably learn this hitch before any other, but often makes the mistake of putting on too many crossing turns. This is unnecessary, because the final hitch will grip the line firmly enough.

The hitch should not be used to make fast sheets, especially on a dinghy, where the line may have to be released from load in a hurry.

Sheepshank

The sheepshank is a knot used for shortening a line, and is rarely found aboard yachts. It does, however, have its uses as shown in the accompanying picture.

First you have to determine how much shorter you want the line to be. Make two bights in the form of a Z with the excess and form two eyes, one at each end of the Z, with the free ends on the underside of the eye in both cases.

Push the lower bight through the left eye, the upper bight through the right eye, and pull the eyes tight. The sheepshank will untie itself if the strain comes off, so if it is likely to be a semi-permanenent fixture it is worth securing the ends of each bight to the standing part with a seizing. The chief advantage of the sheepshank is that it can be made in the middle of a line that is secured at both ends.

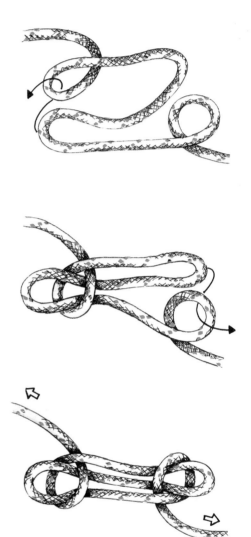

The most important function of this knot is the shortening of a rope that is too long, but you can also call on it in an emergency when, for example, you see a section of the rope that looks as though it is just about to give way. If you make a sheepshank with the dicey part in the middle you can gain yourself time to make up a new line in relative peace. It is not recommended for use in halyards or sheets, even in an emergency, since it is too bulky to run through a block.

Loop knot

The loop knot is a shortening technique, like the sheepshank, but as easy to make as the half hitch.

Sometimes it will provide an instant remedy, in an emergency, enabling you to bypass a section of line that seems in danger of breaking, or to shorten a line immediately. It is very safe, provided that it is well tightened. The main advantage of this knot lies in the fact that it can be made very quickly and can be learnt simply. It is, however, difficult to release once a strain has been put on it.

To make it, double up the rope so that you have a bight with the poor section in the middle of the bight. Form an eye and push the end of the bight through, then pull the knot tight. Under load the damaged section of rope will be strain-free.

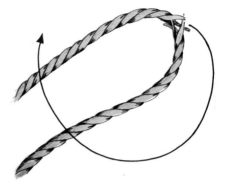

If you have a line that looks to be in imminent danger of breaking, you will have to be able to make a knot in seconds that will prevent it from parting. The sheepshank would do, but would take too long to make. The main disadvantage to the loop knot is that it cannot be made in a line under tension, and that is when you are most likely to need it — such as with warps.

It is worth remembering that the knot is very difficult to release once it has been under load; on the other hand you won't be able to use the damaged end of the line once it has broken. If you want to splice the two parts together, you will have to shorten the line.

Heaving line knot

A practical, good-looking knot that can be
used to thicken a rope's end so that it doesn't
slip through a block, but in the main is used
to weight the end of a line so that it can be
thrown. Simply made and fairly simple to
undo, it firms up in use and is unlikely to
untie itself.

Make a bight and take a turn round the
standing part with the free end. Then take
several more turns, one next to the other,
gradually working closer towards the apex of
the bight. Once you have enough turns round
the standing part to give the knot the
required weight, pass the free end through
the end of the bight. Pull the free end tight,
then pull on the standing part so that the
bight grips the end.

When making the turns round the bight,
keep some tension up as you wind round, or
you might find the half-finished knot falling
apart.

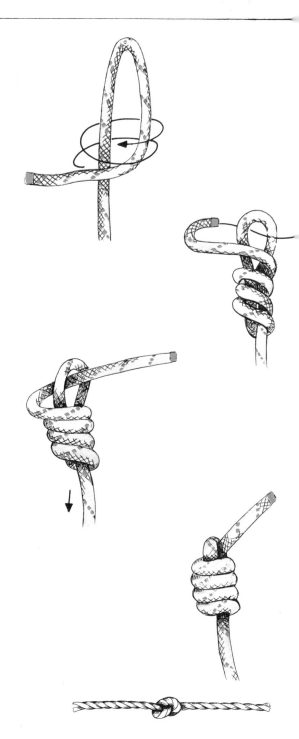

This knot is simpler and faster to make than a monkey's fist and does the same job. It can also be used in place of a figure of eight knot, or even to shorten a line without cutting it, as the turns take up quite a length of line.

Waggoner's hitch

A useful, practical knot, the waggoner's hitch
makes it possible to heave tight a line yet
leave it ready for immediate release. It is
therefore eminently suitable for securing
items of deck gear or for hauling down
halyards towards the guardrail so that they
don't frap against the mast while berthed.

Tie a half hitch in the middle of the line in
such a way that the knot forms a loop as
shown; the best way of doing this is to make
an eye in the line with the free end over and
on top of the standing part, then push
through a reasonable-sized bight. Pull the
knot tight.

Now lead the free end down to the fitting
you want to secure the line to. Take a
half-turn round the fitting, bring the free end
back up and through the loop, then back
down again to the fitting. Heave tight and
secure with a half hitch.

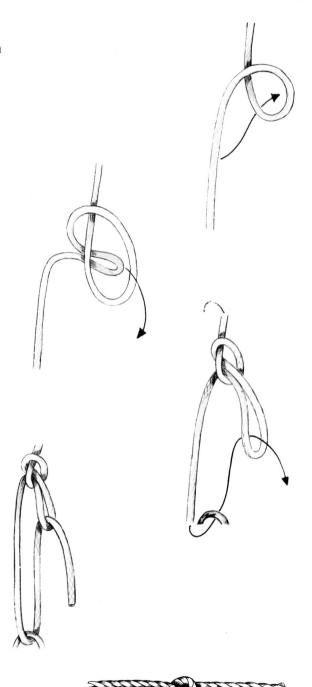

There are many uses for the waggoner's hitch both on land and at sea, whenever you have to heave tight a lashing and have neither the time nor the equipment with which to rig a tackle. In addition to this function, the hitch will also serve as a jury-rigged purchase (a form of tackle) to reduce almost by half the effort required to lift a load. The drawback in this instance is that the free end will very quickly rub through the rope at the loop, so it should only be used as a temporary expedient.

Fishing hook hitch

Many different knots are used to tie hooks to fishing lines, but this is one of the best. Broadly similar to the heaving line knot in conception, it is formed in the same way: you pull the line down parallel with the shank of the hook, form an eye and make several turns of the line end through the eye and round the hook. The number of turns needed is something you will learn by experience; a rough guide is that, after pulling tight, the knot will cover about a quarter of the length of the hook.

Once you have arrived at enough turns, pull the knot tight so that each turn sits firmly against the next without riding up over it. If you have miscalculated and there is still a long tail to the free end, cut it off. If you don't, it may scare off the fish.

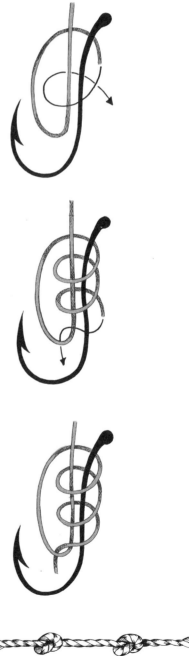

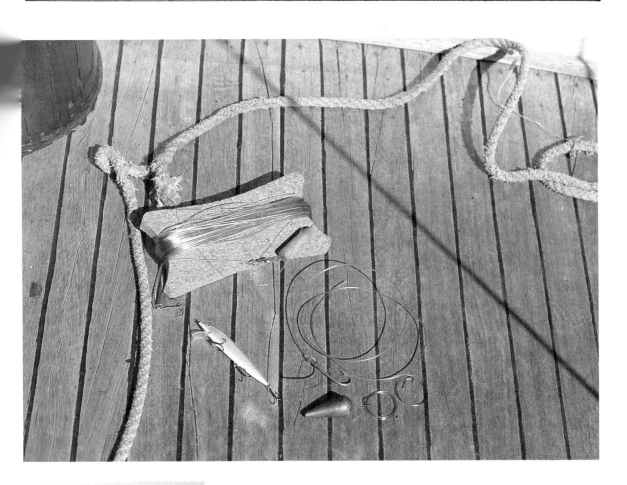

Nowadays many fishing hooks are sold complete with ready-made eyes to attach lines to, but you should nevertheless learn this knot for use when you need one of the older, larger but rarely used hooks that can be found in every angler's locker. This same method comes in handy for securing hooks that have a flange on the shank instead of an eye.

Reef knot

The method most commonly used to join two rope ends of equal size is the reef knot. Once made, it is adequately secure, yet grips even tighter as the line comes under tension. Sometimes it can prove difficult to undo, especially with thin lines and with wet lines that have been subjected to considerable strain.

The reef knot causes some trouble for beginners, who often tend to make it the wrong way round and form the so-called granny knot.

The reef knot proper is symmetrical — the granny isn't — and consists of twin overhand knots. Make one overhand, and note which of the two rope ends is uppermost (the one on the left, coloured white, in the top picture). To form the second overhand, lay the uppermost end (white) over the other, which is then passed through the eye so formed. If you remember 'right over left and twist, then left over right and twist', you will never get it wrong.

To pull the knot tight, pull on both standing parts at the same time.

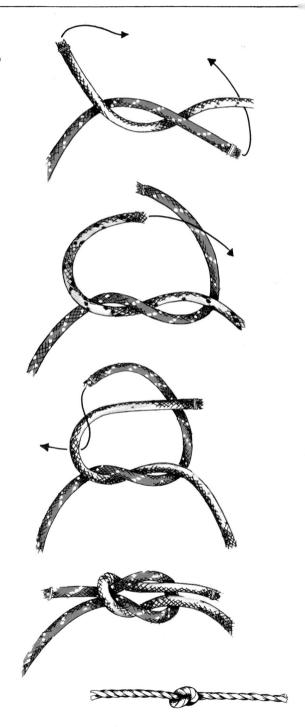

The reef knot can be used in various situations, whenever you have to join two lines of roughly equal thickness. It is not recommended for ropes widely differing in diameter, where a sheetbend will prove more secure. It is still used for the purpose after which it was named, for tying reef points on sails, but often in the slipped form (see overleaf). Other uses: tying battens into their pockets, securing gear on deck, or lengthening a warp by joining it to another. The knot is sometimes secured with a half hitch on each free end.

Slipped reef knot

This variation on the foregoing knot has the advantage that it is easily released even when wet and under load. The only difference between the two is that the slipped knot has one rope end tucked back to form a bight. When you have to release the knot, simply pull on this end.

Start with an overhand knot, as with the conventional reef knot, but this time form a loop with the underlying line (the right hand end in the second picture) and use the loop to make the second overhand knot. The same rule of 'right over left, left over right' still applies.

Another way of making this knot is to form a reef knot and then tuck one of the free ends back inside.

The slipped reef knot is chiefly used to tie reef points on the mainsail, which are often subjected to considerable loads and frequently soaked through by rain and spray. The knot used has to be easy to release when you want to shake out the reef. The only point to watch for is that it should be pulled tight, so that it doesn't work loose with the pressure on the sail.

It is therefore used in place of the reef knot whenever there might be a need to release the knot in a hurry.

Sheetbend

The sheetbend — or signal halyard bend, as it is known when used to tie together thin lines — is particularly suited to situations where two lines of differing diameters are to be joined. It works on a similar principle to the blackwall hitch.

Make a bight with the thicker of the two lines, so that it takes the shape of an eye splice; then thread the thinner one under and into the bight, round the standing part and the free end of the thicker line and back under its own standing part, so that it grips tight.

If you pass the end of the thinner line round the bight a second time, then tuck it through its own standing part once more, you will have made a double sheetbend, which is more secure and in many cases to be preferred as a single sheetbend does not grip well in synthetic rope.

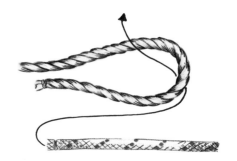

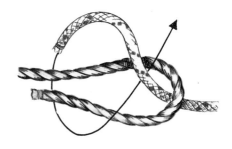

This is another knot with many uses. Its most common purpose in life is to join together two lines to make one long one — especially when one of those lines has a ready-made loop or eye in the end. In the majority of such cases the double sheetbend will be more suitable than the reef knot.

The single sheetbend is often found in signal halyards, where it is used to attach the halyard to the eye on the flag hoist. It is easy to make and release, and holds securely. For general purposes, the sheetbend's main advantage lies in the fact that it is ideal for tying together thin lines that would jam if joined with a reef knot.

Double thumb knot

Rarely used by yachtsmen, the double thumb knot (thumb knot is another name for overhand) is nevertheless ideal for those cases where two ropes or hawsers have to be joined together absolutely securely. The greater the load, the stronger it grips.

Start by making an overhand knot in one of the two ends. Take the second rope and simply follow the course of the first in reverse to form a second overhand knot adjacent and parallel to the original. Pull both knots tight.

It is worth seizing each of the free ends on to the standing part of the opposite rope, as shown.

This knot is particularly valuable when you have to join two heavy ropes that are likely to come under a lot of strain, such as the mooring lines of bigger craft.

If the ropes are old and pliable or of very different diameters it is best to choose another knot, as this one can be very difficult to undo.

Carrick bend

Of the many different techniques available
for joining two lines together, the carrick
bend comes second only to the splice in
security. It is also simple to make and quick
to release.

Form an eye in one of the two ropes in
such a way that the free end lies below the
standing part (in the picture the free end of
the white rope is the one shown leading out
of the picture towards top left). Lay the other
(blue) line underneath this eye, and lead its
free end over the standing part of the first
line, under the free end and back towards the
eye. Now tuck it into the eye, under its own
standing part, and out of the eye again to
form a symmetrical shape. This symmetry is
lost when the strain comes on the line, but
the bend remains easy to undo.

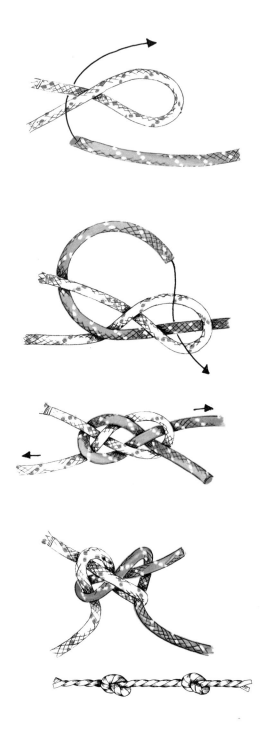

The carrick bend is not very well known, although it has all the qualities of a good knot: it is reliable, won't undo itself and yet remains easy to release even after being strained. Used to join heavy lines, tow lines, mooring warps and anchor warps, it can also replace the reef knot in some situations, although it requires a little more care in the making.

Reeving line bend

This knot is used to join together two relatively thick lines, such as mooring warps, without preventing them from running freely over a bow roller or other fitting. It consists of twin half hitches secured with a seizing each, and is therefore somewhat time-consuming to make. For this reason, it is best only to adopt the reeving line bend when the join is likely to be more or less permanent.

The reliability of the bend depends on the care taken in fixing the seizings. The two rope ends are laid parallel and in the opposite direction to one another, and the tail of each is formed into a half hitch around the other. This is secured with a seizing in each case so that both half hitches are equally tight.

This bend is one method of securing two lines, in cases where a splice for one reason or another is impractical, with a knot that is not too bulky. The reeving line bend (so called because it is used on lines that have to be rove through a fairlead) is therefore appropriate for anchor warps, mooring warps and hawsers that have to be led through fairleads or wound onto a winch drum.

Bowline bend

The bowline bend is used on those occasions where you need to join a couple of lines totally securely and in a hurry. It is considerably more reliable than either the sheetbend or the reef knot.

   The knot consists of two interlinked bowlines made one after the other, so that the loop of the second passes through the loop of the first. The more strain is put on the lines, the stronger the join.

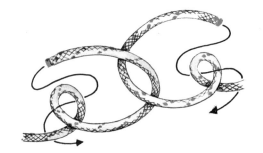

This knot is used to tie together two rope ends that are likely to be subjected to heavy loading. You might choose it on board when you suddenly discover that the line you wanted to use is too short and you have to bend on another fast.

It is not suitable for situations where the rope ends are likely to have to pass through a deck eye or a block, as the bowline doesn't taper and is a relatively bulky knot.

True lovers' knot

This knot is used in the main to join together
two fishing lines that are too thin to accept a
reef knot or sheetbend without slipping. It
consists of an overhand knot in each line,
formed in such a way that they slide together
and grip tight. This is by far the best method
of joining very thin lines, but is difficult to
undo after it has come under tension.

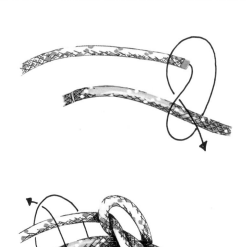

The two ends are laid parallel and in
opposite directions, and each is formed into
an overhand knot around the other so that
the line on the left is knotted around the line
on the right and vice versa.

To secure the join, haul on both standing
parts until the knots are butted hard up
against each other.

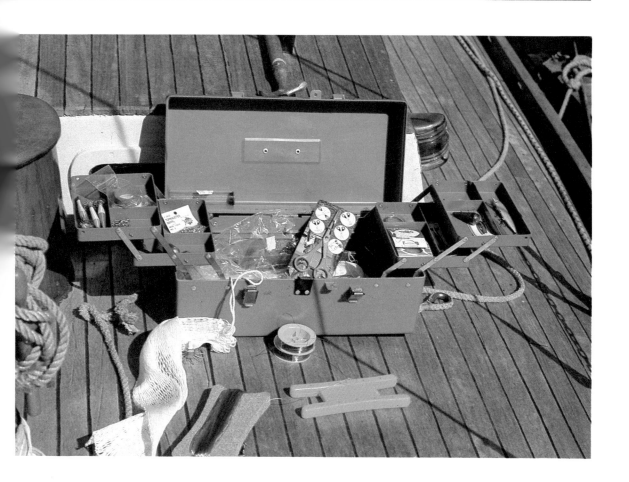

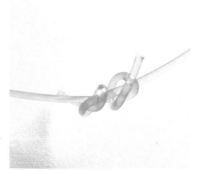

As we have already said, this knot is mostly used to join two thin lines. Correctly made and, most importantly, fully drawn together, it will hold the finest of nylon fishing lines.

A similar knot can be made using two figure of eights; it is somewhat bulkier, but easier to undo.

Stopper hitch

Sometimes it may be necessary to hold or move a line under strain, such as a mooring warp, a sheet or a halyard. For this you need another short length of line called a stopper, made up with a rolling hitch around the bigger line.

With the free end of the stopper take a turn round the warp, sheet or halyard so that the end lies over the standing part as shown in the top picture. Take another turn round the warp, again riding over the standing part, and follow this with a half hitch around the part of the warp that is to remain under tension.

The knot will hold tight under strain, but only in one direction. If the warp or sheet is particularly smooth you can add another couple of round turns before finishing the rolling hitch off with the half hitch. The stopper can be released under strain by simply undoing the half hitch.

This is a temporary knot that can be used in a hurry. It is more reliable as a long-term fixture if secured with a seizing (see page 38).

There are times when strong winds or tide make it impossible to release a warp. This is the correct circumstance in which to use a stopper: tie a rolling hitch around the warp, lead the stopper to a winch or windlass and use the power to take the strain off the warp end so that it can be released.

A stopper on the genoa sheet takes the strain off the fairlead and makes it possible to adjust its position.

The stopper holds of its own accord when under tension. As the tension eases it can be released by hand.

West Country whipping

This knotted whipping is used relatively
seldom, as it is neither as firm nor as
attractive as the other form of whipping. It is
worth using as a temporary expedient, for
instance to hold the strands of a rope
together in order to splice.

A West Country whipping is very quick to
make. Take a turn round the rope with the
twine and form the first overhand knot,
ensuring that the two ends of twine left are of
roughly equal length. Take another half turn
around the rope with each length of twine
and form a second overhand knot on the
other side of the rope, and so on in such a
way that the knots alternate all the way up
the rope. Finish off with a reef knot, in other
words two overhand knots one on top of the
other. The whipping should be pulled tight at
each stage so that it grips uniformly.

Whippings are designed to prevent loose ends of a rope from unravelling. There are two basic types, permanent and temporary; the West Country whipping is one of the latter, often put on a rope before splicing in order to hold the strands together while the first tucks are made. It can be removed easily once the splice is complete.

The same method can also be adopted to whip stock rope stowed for future use, where the relative weakness of the whipping doesn't matter.

Common whipping

Somewhat more complex than the previous
whipping, this form is still easy to make and
practical, as no needle is needed.

Make a bight with the end of the twine and
lay it along the rope to be whipped in the
direction of the rope end. Take a series of
turns around the rope, gradually working
towards the rope end, ensuring that the turns
are laid hard against each other without
riding up. Also take care that the bight
remains securely gripped.

When the whipping approaches the end of
the rope, tuck the twine through the top of
the bight and pull the twine at the other end
of the whipping so that the bight is hauled
down to the middle of the whipping. Cut off
the loose ends of twine close against the
turns.

With artificial fibre ropes the strands of the
rope can be sealed with a soldering iron.

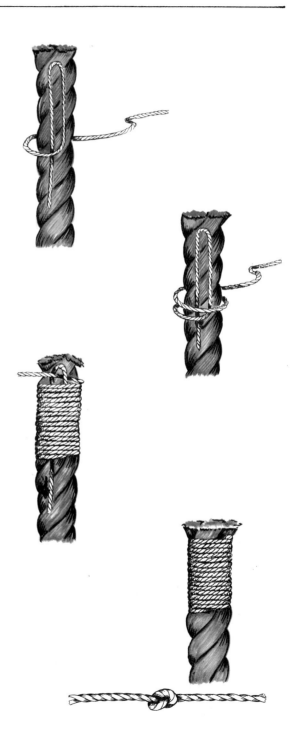

Easily made and useful though it may be, the common whipping does have one major drawback; when the rope end becomes wet and swells, it stretches the twine, which on drying again may slip off. It is therefore best not to rely on this form of whipping for ropes that are in frequent use unless you are prepared to keep renewing it.

Palm-and-needle whipping

This whipping is especially suited to twisted rope. You will need a sailmaker's needle with an eye big enough to take the twine.

Begin by inserting the needle through the rope at the point where you want the whipping to start. Push the needle through a strand, rather than between, so that the knotted end of the twine is held firmly, and begin successive turns in the same way as for a common whipping.

Once you have enough turns on the rope, push the needle through a strand so that it exits in the gap between two strands. Follow this gap (known as the score) down to the lower end of the whipping, and insert the needle once again so that it exits in the score between the next two strands. Follow the score up and repeat, so that you end up with a diagonal line of twine, called frapping turns, running down between each pair of strands. Finally, push the needle under the whipping again, pull the twine through and cut off the end.

If the rope is braided rather than twisted, you can still put in the frapping turns as if there were the usual strands.

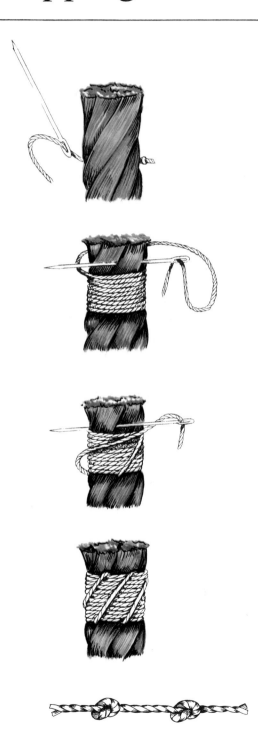

Palm-and-needle whipping is often used to secure the ends of boltropes, as it stands up well to friction. This type of whipping is both durable and reliable, but needs some practice. With hard-laid rope you may have to open up a hole for the needle with a fid.

Use the whipping wherever the rope is in common or heavy use or subject to friction. Running rigging in particular, which is led through blocks, is a good example of where to use it.

Snaked whipping

The best whipping of all, this is also the most attractive-looking. Needless to say, it is also the most difficult to make.

You need a sailmaker's needle and a sailmaker's palm. It bears some resemblance to the previous version, and is equally well suited to twisted rope, although you will more often see it used on braided line.

Start as you would with the palm-and-needle whipping. When you have wound on the last turn, however, pull the needle through the rope and haul tight; then thread the needle between the last and the second-from-last turn of the whipping, and follow the line of the strands down to the opposite end of the whipping. Repeat the exercise, up one way and down the other, in such a way that every diagonal crosses behind the previous one (see the third picture). Finish off with two half-hitches, push the needle through the rope once again; pull the twine tight and cut the end off close.

It is a good idea to pick up a few fibres of the rope itself on the first and last turns around the whipping, which makes the snaking less likely to slip.

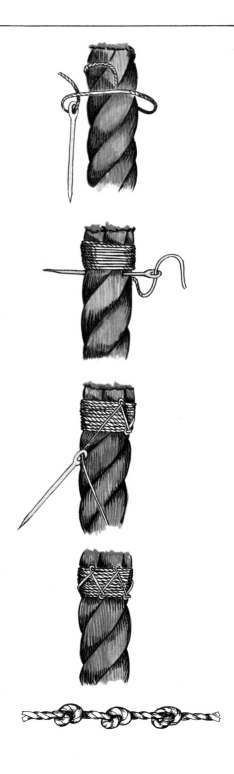

We have already said all there is to say about the purpose and making of this whipping, but it is worth reiterating that any whipping is only effective if every turn is pulled taut. The snaked whipping is ideal for finishing off the ends of large-diameter lines; with thinner lines it is very difficult to make.

You can also use snaked whipping as the basis for seizing, in which case you will not be trying to hold the strands of a single line together, but a pair of lines. Because it looks so good, snaked whipping is often used on lines that are left out on board, such as sheets.

Double wall knot

You will often see aboard yachts warps, halyards or sheets whose ends have been tied with a half hitch to prevent the strands unravelling or the end from slipping through a block. The double wall knot, sometimes called the rose knot, is in such cases considerably more durable and more attractive. Nor is it that difficult to make.

Unravel the strands a few inches and put on a temporary whipping. Make a loop with each strand as shown in the first diagram, inserting the end of the first strand through the loop in the second, the end of the second through the loop in the third and the end of the third through the loop in the first. Pull each strand tight, and you have a single wall knot. Now repeat the knot by following each strand round a second time so that you form a second wall knot on top of the first. Finish off by threading the ends of each strand through the centre and trimming them close to the end of the rope, or alternatively putting on a whipping.

If the double wall knot doesn't come out right, swop the strands around for the second circuit of the rope, and the mistake will be obvious.

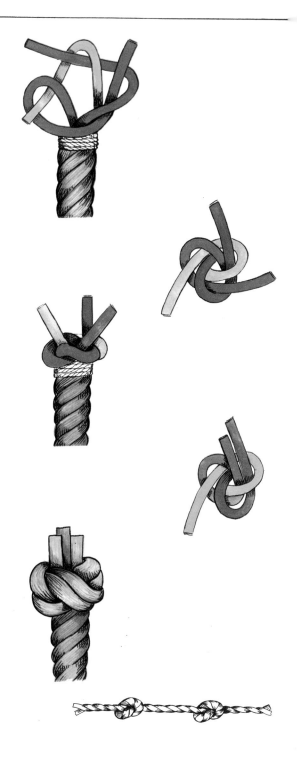

This knot can only be made in stranded rope, not in braided. It will serve as a whipping, and prevent the rope from unravelling, but is also often found on the fall of a halyard, where it prevents the end of the line slipping through and disappearing up the mast.

Matthew Walker knot

This is a concealed knot made from the strands of a rope end, and is designed to stop the rope end from unravelling. The knot demands a certain dexterity and some practice. Once made it is either trimmed off or whipped; alternatively the strands can be combed out flat to make a wide tassle or paintbrush shape.

Start by unravelling the end of the rope, then take the first strand, take a turn round the end of the rope and thread the strand through its own bight, as shown on the left in the top picture.

Take the second strand and take another turn round the rope end, then thread it through the bights formed by both the first and second strands. The same procedure is repeated with the third strand, which is inserted through the bights formed by the first and second strands before being threaded through its own bight. Pull the strands taut so that the knot looks like the one shown in the bottom picture.

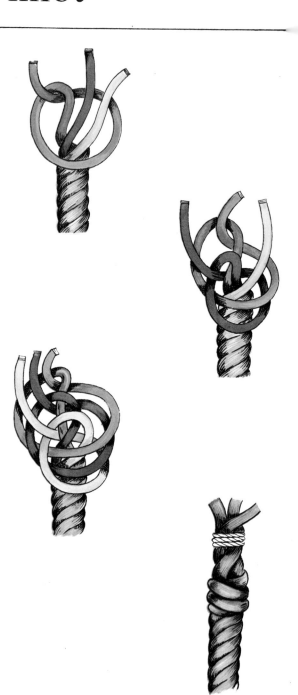

On board yachts ropes in natural fibre are rarely used nowadays, and the only three-stranded line is usually made of nylon or of polypropylene. The Matthew Walker knot, however, is still very useful, as it prevents the end of such ropes from unravelling or slipping through a block. Many sailors might prefer to heat up the rope end so that the fibres melt and weld together, or to whip the end properly. The Matthew Walker provides a better solution, as it looks much more attractive and is more reliable in the long run. The knot appears on first sight to be more difficult than it is; in fact, it is the first step towards the tricky tasks such as splicing and fancywork.

93

Back splice

This splice is used worldwide, in some countries being called Spanish whipping. It starts with a crown knot, which looks very similar to the wall knot except that the individual strands are led over rather than under their neighbours. Once the knot has been pulled taut the splicing can begin.

Take any one of the strands and lead it round against the lay of the rope, over the next strand and under the third strand. Do the same with the other two strands so that when you have finished the strands are leaving the knot at regular intervals of 120°. Pull the knot tight without losing its shape. Each strand is then taken over the strand of the rope immediately below its exit point and tucked under the next. At least two, preferably three tucks are made with each strand before trimming off the ends (not too close).

To make the job easier, put on a temporary whipping at the point to which you want to unlay the rope. It can be removed once the crown knot has been pulled tight.

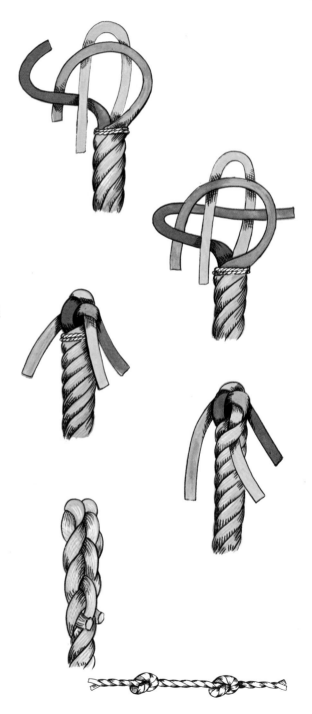

This splice can substitute for whipping in twisted rope, either three- or four-strand. It is decorative and fairly easy to concoct as required. Its main drawback is in making the end of the rope rather bulky, but this may be an advantage in certain circumstances.

Unlike whipping, the back splice becomes firmer and stronger with time, which makes it ideal for use with mooring warps. As with the previous knots a fid will be a great help in separating the strands to take in the tucks.

Flat seizing

Seizing means the binding together of two
ropes with twine or thin line wrapped firmly
round the ropes and pulled tight. Although it
can be used for binding separate lengths, it is
seen most often holding together two parts of
an eye as shown in the illustrations.

Prepare the twine by opening it up and
tucking the end through individual strands a
couple of times as shown in the small
black-and-white drawing. Take a turn round
both ropes and thread the twine back on
itself, then continue round both ropes so that
you make a series of tight turns, one butting
firmly against the next. Finish off by
threading the twine in between the two ropes
and making a series of frapping turns around
the seizing at right angles to the initial turns.
Secure the seizing with a knot or by passing
the end of the twine a couple of times
underneath the vertical turns and pulling
taut.

The simple flat seizing is used to bind a couple of ropes together temporarily, but is not suitable in cases where the join is likely to come under great strain. The palm-and-needle seizing, although more time-consuming and tricky to make, is generally better, but a more permanent and attractive solution is to put on a conventional eye splice.

Palm-and-needle seizing

This form of seizing is in principle the same as the flat version except that you begin by threading the twine through the rope with a sailmaker's needle. This gives it much better grip.

If you are using the seizing to make an eye, start by forming the rope into an eye of the required size. Knot the end of the twine, then thread it through the rope at the point where you want the seizing to start. Pull the twine through. Now insert the needle in the rope again, this time through both ropes at the point where you want the seizing to end, in the opposite direction. Return to the start point, thread the twine through the second rope and begin the seizing turns. Finish off with a few frapping turns, secured by threading the twine underneath the frapping turns before trimming off close.

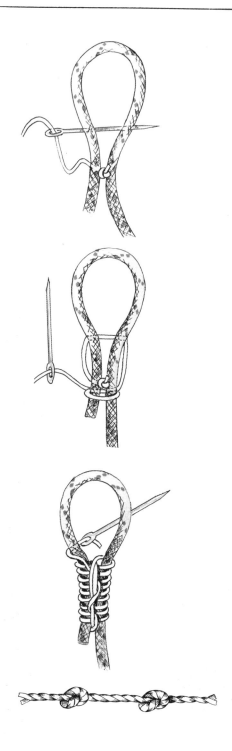

This method of seizing is used to make an eye in the end of a rope. It can be used in conjunction with a thimble for protection from chafe, which is particularly important when the seizing is used on sheets to connect a shackle to a clew.

Palm-and-needle seizings are used wherever the rope is subjected to heavy loads, so it is important to take care to learn the correct technique. The seizing is relatively quick and simple to make and is suitable for making eyes in braided lines.

Short splice

We have now covered a number of knots that can be used to join the ends of two lines. For a permanent join, a short splice is a much better solution.

Put a temporary whipping on both lines, unlay them and then bring them together so that each strand of one line lies between and in the opposite direction to each strand of the other.

Tie the loose strands of one line along the other so that the two lines are held together firmly while you start to splice. Lead one of the remaining loose strands over one strand, under the next, as shown in the third drawing, in such a way that the tuck points in the opposite direction to the lay of the rope.

Do the same with the second and third strands, each of which is led over one, under one. Repeat the whole process at least twice and preferably three times, then remove the temporary seizing holding the other three loose strands and splice them into the other line in the same way. Take care on starting the second splice to pull the first tuck tight so that the two lines are drawn together without a gap between the two splices. Once you have made two or three tucks in the second rope, cut off all six loose ends and push them into the splice or whip them. Finally, roll the splice under the sole of your foot so that it looks neat and uniformly round.

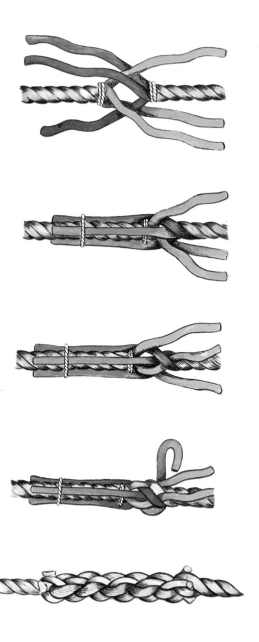

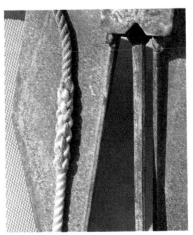

The short splice is used whenever you have to join two ropes permanently together; to repair a break in an otherwise satisfactory line, for example, or to lengthen an anchor or mooring warp.

Made well, this splice is very strong, and is unlikely to unravel of its own accord. As with all splices, there may be a problem if you cut the ends of each strand off too close in an effort to improve the look. These can either be whipped or, in the case of artificial-fibre ropes, heat-welded into the splice.

Long splice

This splice serves the same function as the short splice we have just covered: to join together two lines of similar strength and thickness. Made with care it is almost as reliable as a short splice, but is thinner and less wearing. To make it you have to unlay a considerable length of line, which gives it its name.

The lines are unlaid as for the short splice, except that it would not be excessive to unlay ten turns of each (in the drawing the lines are shown cut short for clarity). Interweave the loose strands between the strands of the other rope, again as for the short splice. The next job is to 'exchange' two strands of each rope for two strands of the other. Start by unlaying one strand a further nine turns back along the rope and lay the corresponding strand of the other rope in the resulting gap; then unlay another nine turns in the opposite direction, and lay the corresponding strand in the gap. The third pair of strands remain as they are. Finally, make an overhand knot with each pair of strands and trim off the ends. The splice has been made correctly if every strand is sitting comfortably in its place. Finish off by tucking each strand into the rope in the direction in which it is pointing.

When relaying the strands along the rope to make the splice, give each a half-twist so that it grips the strands of the other line. Splicing will be easier if you unlay two turns, then relay two turns, and continue until all nine have been exchanged.

It used to be said 'different ship, different long splice', indicating that this form of splice appears in several versions. This is one of the most popular variants.

The long splice is used mainly when it is important that the splice is hardly thicker than the ropes being spliced, for example in the case of a line that has to run through a block. It is not quite as strong as the short splice, but in many cases this disadvantage will be outweighed by the advantage of size.

Splicing wire into twisted rope

In the same way as you can splice two ropes together, you can also splice wire into rope. Properly executed the join will be very strong. Putting on a temporary seizing, unlay the end of the rope, and trim the ends of each strand progressively so that they taper off; then unlay the wire so that the outer loose strands are twice as long as the inner ones. If there is an inner core, cut it off.

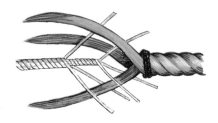

Begin as you would for a short splice, interweaving the three strands of the rope with the inner three strands of wire. Tuck each strand of the wire into the rope and put on a seizing, then continue with another couple of tucks. Repeat the tucks, over one strand, under the next, with the outer wire strands and the tapered rope, finishing off with a second seizing at the point where the rope ends. Cut off the excess wire strands with a pair of pliers and roll the splice under your shoe to shape it. Finally put a whipping — in this case, termed a serving — over the whole splice from end to end.

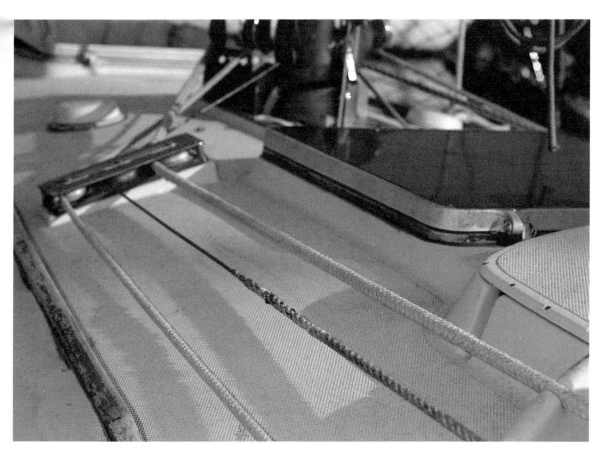

A wire halyard, obviously, cannot be wound on to a small winch or cleated, so in both circumstances you would need a rope tail spliced into the wire.

A splice of this sort will, however, be the weak link in a line, so it should be regularly checked for wear and strength.

Splicing wire into braided rope

Before beginning the splice, you will have to prepare both ends. Cut the wire diagonally into a point and wrap insulating tape around the tapered end so that it will slide into the rope without any of the strands catching. Now take the rope, and tie a knot about 5 ft (1.5 m) from the end. Cut 8 in (20 cm) or so from the outer sheath, then push it back as far as it will go so that it bunches up against the knot. Insert the end of the wire into the centre of the rope and push well in — 2 ft (60 cm) for preference.

Now wrap the inner core of the rope with insulating tape some 6 in (15 cm) from the end and unpick the braid to this point. You can then make the loose yarns into three false strands with insulating tape as shown in the second picture. With a Swedish spike splice the 'strands' into the wire, with each strand tucked under two strands of the wire. Take at least four tucks with each strand. Then trim off the rope strands (without using heat). Let the outer sheath slide back into its normal position, wrap insulating tape round the sheath 6 in (15 cm) from the end, unpick the braid as you did with the core and form it into three separate strands. Splice these into the wire. This time, after two tucks cut through half of each strand so that it begins to taper. After the third tuck reduce the diameter by half once again, and after the fourth tuck cut the strands off close against the wire.

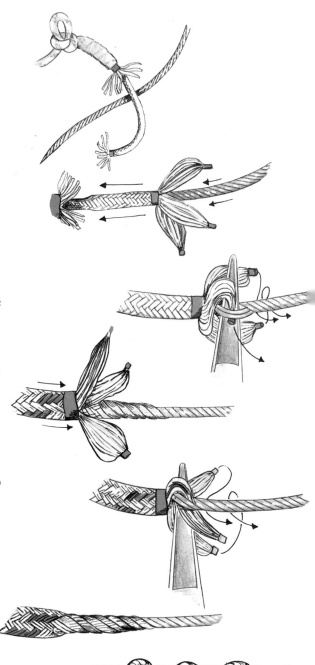

Nowadays sixty per cent of the ropes used on board are braided, so it is very important to master this splice. It may seem difficult, but it isn't once you know how to splice three-strand rope. Its purpose is the same as that of the other wire-rope splice we have described. Its main advantage is that the wire remains relatively unharmed with its strength unimpaired throughout its length, yet still grips the rope well.

Eye splice

The eye splice is the most reliable method there is of making an eye in the end of a rope. Unlay the end and put on a temporary whipping. Then form an eye of the required size and tuck one of the loose strands under one of the strands of the standing part so that it is at right angles to the lay of the rope.

Thread the second strand under the neighbouring strand of the standing part, still in the same direction; then turn the eye round and tuck the third loose strand under the only strand in the standing part that has not yet been used. All three strands should be hauled tight. Take off the whipping and put in another two tucks. When the splice is complete, roll it between the hands or under the feet and trim off the ends.

You will always need eyes in the end of your ropes. Splices like the one shown are strong, will never undo themselves and will last a long time if protected from chafe by a thimble. They can be used on permanent mooring warps, on the ends of sheets, halyards, kicking straps — anything made of three-strand rope.

The greenest of green sailors should have the eye splice in his catalogue of skills, as it's easier to make than many knots.

Eye splice in wire

An eye splice in wire is no more difficult than a splice in rope, it will just require more work. One difficulty is that the wire strands are less easy to manipulate. You will need a marlin spike, a wooden mallet, twine and a thimble.

It is a good idea to wear gloves to avoid risk of injury; to achieve a more professional result, you will also need a good pair of pliers to pull the strands through after each tuck.

Form the eye around the thimble and secure it with a temporary seizing. Unlay the strands as far as the seizing and cut back the core to the same point. Now lay three of the loose strands on top of the standing part, the other three underneath. Insulating tape wrapped round each end should make the job easier. Each strand should be tucked under the neighbouring strand — or preferably the next two strands — of the standing part in the direction of the lay. (For the sake of clarity the simpler method has been shown.) For the second tuck each strand should be led over one, under one. Repeat for another four tucks, for the last tuck using only half the thickness of wire in each strand so that the splice tapers towards the end. Finally beat the splice into shape with the mallet to close up the strands and ensure that they grip tight, then cover the splice with a serving.

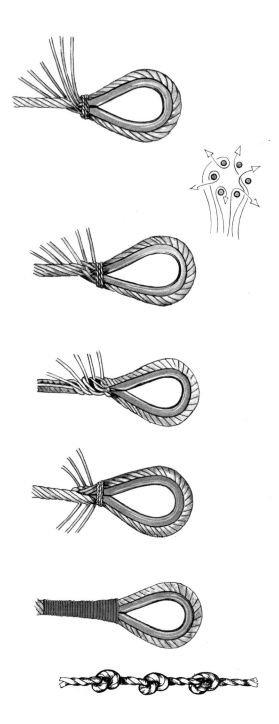

There are many uses for an eye splice in the rigging of a small boat where you don't want to go to the expense of highly-priced terminals: attaching shrouds and stays to bottlescrews, joining halyards to rope tails. To give the eye its correct shape and prevent the wire from rubbing through the rope, a thimble is invariably used.

Sleeve-swaged terminals

These terminals are very popular and used widely, as they need a single fairly cheap tool that has a place in every tool kit. The drawback is that a hand-pressed terminal is of only limited strength. It might be adequate for a small boat, but not, for example, on the genoa halyard of a blue-water yacht.

You will need a sleeve of the right size so that the wire will just slip through. The wire is passed through the sleeve and back again to form an eye. Insert a thimble in the eye so that it is held tightly and pull the wire taut so that the apex of the thimble butts up against the sleeve. Now compress the sleeve in the swager, steadily increasing the pressure as you work away from the eye. The sharp edges left by the press should be filed off without damaging the rest of the sleeve. Make sure that the terminal is as clean as possible, so as to prevent the build-up of rust.

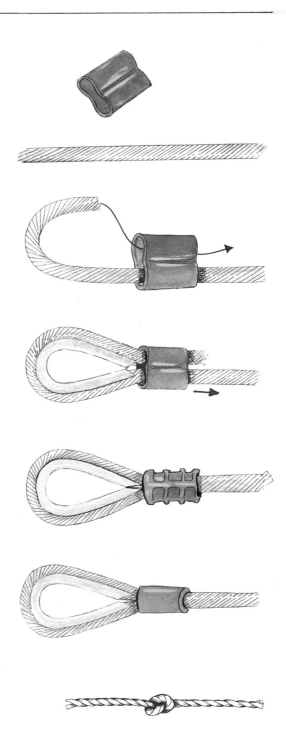

As has already been said, swaged terminals are extremely practical in the rigging of a small boat. It is very difficult, however, to forecast the breaking strain of a hand-pressed terminal. This will depend on the type of sleeve, the strength of the wire, the type of press and the care taken by the fitter.

The Norseman terminal

The Norseman and similar makes of terminal
are used to join a prefabricated eye to a wire
shroud. They are ideal for 1×19 and 7×7
stainless steel wire, and offer one of the most
effective do-it-yourself methods of securing
standing rigging. To assemble a Norseman,
insert the wire into the end of the terminal.
Spread the outer strands of wire apart, so
that they unlay themselves, then push the
cone-shaped wedge along the inner core as
far as it will go. Hold the outer wire strands
tightly against the cone as you screw the eye
into the end of the terminal. Secure by
tightening the nut up against the terminal.

It is very important that the terminal is the
right size for the wire. With the different
ways used to measure wire and terminals, it is
not always easy to be sure.

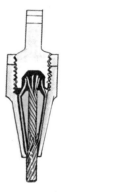

Norseman terminals offer a good solution to the problem of attaching standing rigging to mast and deck eyes. They can be fitted with tools usually found on board and are more durable than swaged terminals. Some varieties will even grip stainless steel rod rigging firmly.

Their disadvantage is that they become less reliable under heavy load. They must, as has been said, be exactly the right size. Finally, you should not use stainless steel terminals for galvanised wire, as the wire will begin to corrode electro-lytically, with obvious consequences.

Monkey's fist

This knot is simple to make and a useful way of weighting the end of a line. The thicker the line, the heavier the knot.

Start by making three full turns in the line as shown, then take the end and make a further three turns around and at right angles to the first three. Bring the end inside the first coil made and take another three turns round the second coil.

Insert the end of the rope into the middle of the knot and start to pull all the turns tight, one after the other. To make a round monkey's fist that is going to stay round, put a small ball in the middle.

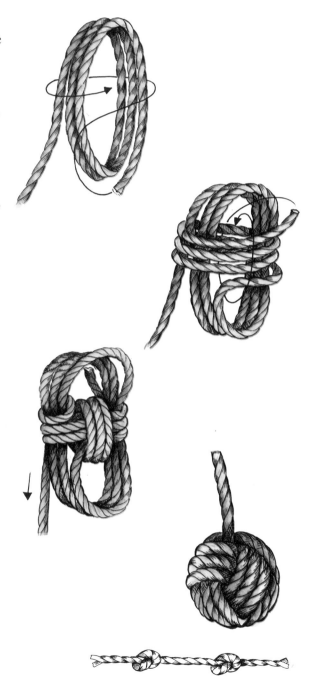

The monkey's fist is designed to lend weight to the end of a heaving line used when mooring, so that the line can be thrown ashore even from some distance away. But it is also used on the end of ropes in place of a back splice, or even as a key fob (in which case you should put a cork ball in the middle, so that it floats if dropped in the water). There are many other uses for this easy-to-make attractive knot.

Turk's Head

In general this fancywork knot is used on thick ropes or tubing to mark a particular spot. You need marline, thin line or leather lacing. The Turk's Head is a decorative knot and looks seamanlike, quite apart from its functional value. The name comes from its similarity to a turban. The pictures show how to make it far better than a lengthy description can; to make the process clearer, the line last used in each illustration is the one coloured light.

For stages 5 and 8 the knot is shown as seen from below so that you can see the part being worked on.

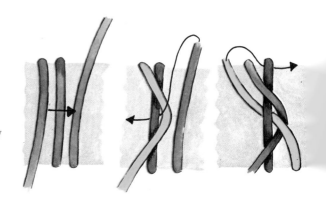

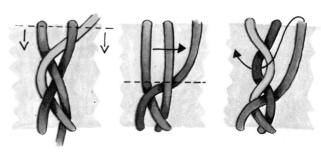

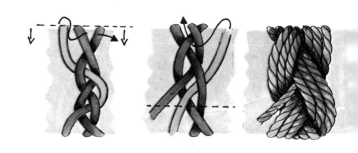

One example of where the Turk's Head might be used is the wheel, where it is often put on to mark the position of centre rudder. It can also be used to decorate a tiller or to hold in position an anti-chafe plastic sleeve on a rope. You can even wrap one round a napkin ring.

With the Turk's Head you can prove that your boat is owned by a seaman.

Deck mat

Less of a knot, more of an example of sailor's handiwork, this is nevertheless a useful accessory. If you want to make one of a specific size, mark out the outside dimensions first of all on the floor with chalk. It is a good idea to have handy a few weights or stones so that you can hold the end in place.

To get a good result, work slowly and without rushing, and concentrate on following exactly all the steps as shown in the illustrations. Once you have completed the mat, you can secure the ends with seizings so that they do not work loose.

Always make two, preferably three or even four, turns.

Mats like this are easy to make out of old, superannuated rope, although ones made out of new rope look rather more appealing.

It is all but impossible to describe the procedure. Simply follow the steps shown in the drawings, which speak for themselves. As with the description of the Turk's Head the strand last used has been coloured yellow.

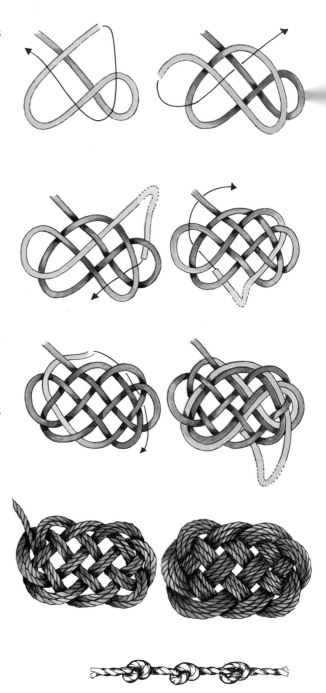

120

Anyone who regularly washes the deck of his boat will know what a huge amount of dirt can collect on deck. Most is brought on board underneath people's shoes. Although many would like to think that rubber soles prevent damage to the deck, it simply isn't so. Even the softest sole can scratch glassfibre if it has picked up a stone.

For this reason the sensible owner will put out a mat on which his guests can clean their shoes before coming on board. The smallest self-made mat will do for the purpose, quite aside from the fact that it helps to make the boat look seamanlike.

Sailmaker's darn

Strictly speaking, sailmaker's needlework does not come within the scope of ropework, but we felt it should be included in this book as the repair of a torn sail or dodger is a necessary aspect of occasional maintenance work on board.

There are several ways of carrying out such a repair, but for simple tears the sailmaker's darn is especially useful.

Start the stitching some way in front of the tear. Knot the end of the twine and pull it through, leaving the tail running parallel with the tear. Make three stitches, so that the second stitch holds the tail of the twine. Then, working from the other side of the sail (the sail is as seen from the other side in the centre picture) make a diagonal stitch through the edge of the tear and back to the facing side. Make a perpendicular stitch across the tear. The next diagonal stitch should be led behind the perpendicular so that it comes out on the other side of the sail, forming a sort of half hitch, before continuing the diagonal. Do not run too close to the edge of the tear with the line of stitches, which should remain parallel with the tear throughout. Continue until you reach the end of the tear, make another three normal stitches and knot the end of the twine. Make sure that the twine is not hauled too tight; the sailcloth should remain flat.

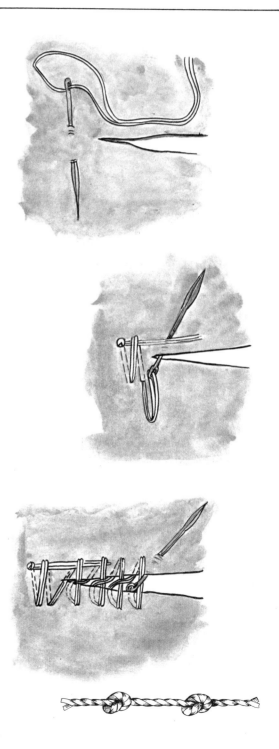

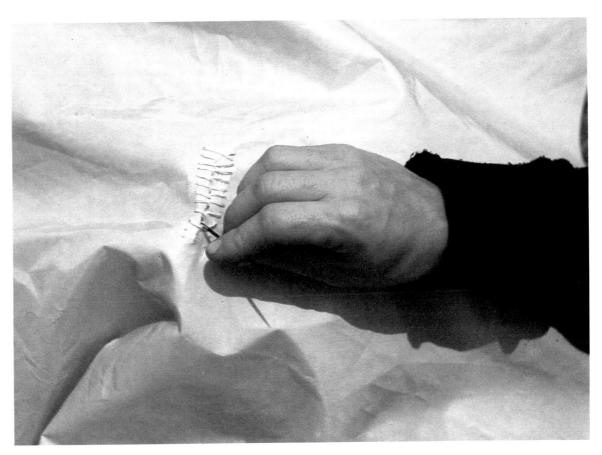

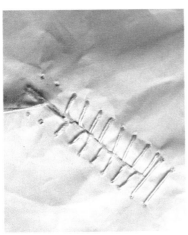

The sailmaker's darn is useful when the tear is not too big and when it runs more or less straight. Tears like this are usually caused by a loose strand of wire from a shroud. If you just want to put on a patch, ordinary stitching will be adequate and there will be no need to cross-stitch. So that you can work with both hands, it is worth putting some sticky tape on the underside of the sail so that the tear is closed up while you sew. The patch should be much larger than the tear, but should not extend over the edge of one of the sail panels into the next. Sew the patch on so firmly that it lies flat, then turn the sail over and stitch up the tear.

Safety netting

A net on the guardrail that will prevent the foresail from slipping overboard is a very worthwhile accessory. To make one you will need a reel of good netting twine about 2/3 mm in diameter, a net needle and a piece of wood with straight sides. Start with a row of loops over the guardrail (the netting can simply be looped over, as shown, or it can be secured at each apex with a clove hitch). To this first row attach a second row of bights, securing them at each apex with a sheetbend. The wooden straight-edge will enable you to check that the mesh is coming out level. Although you can make a net by hand alone, it is advisable to have a net needle, which will save you having to pull the whole line through at each turn. If the foredeck has no toerail to fasten the bottom of the net to, secure the bottom row to a line stretched between a stanchion and the pulpit.

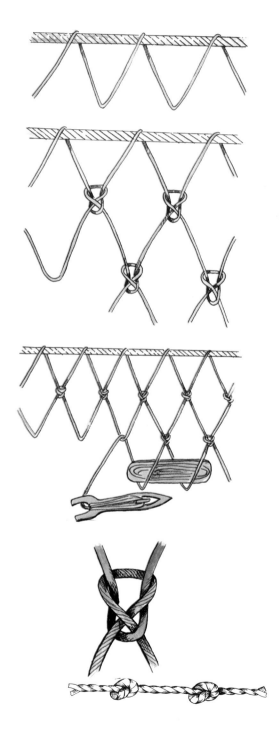

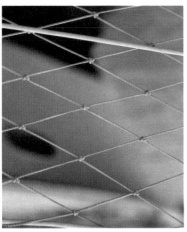

Safety netting simplifies foredeck work and stops a sail slipping between the guardrail and the deck and falling into the water. It goes without saying that a foresail that falls overboard will slow the boat down, and it will also often be difficult to retrieve. A net like this is also to be recommended when children are on board, in which case it should be extended all the way to the stern.

Coiling a rope

Coiling is not just a matter of forming a rope into a series of loops so that it can be stowed; its main function is to ensure that the rope will be immediately to hand, untangled, when it is needed again. The bights can be made either in the hand or, in the case of a heavy rope, on the deck.

To get the right results, hold the coils in one hand and make new ones with the other. A right-hand-laid rope should always be coiled clockwise. To avoid snagging, give each loop a light twist before taking it in hand; a right-hand-laid rope should be twisted to the right, a left-hand one to the left. With the last part of the line take a couple of turns round the whole coil, insert the end of the rope through the hole at the top and pull through. The turns will slide up and grip the end.

All ropes and lines on board must be properly coiled before they are stowed or put aside for future use. Mooring lines, in particular, should be coiled while not in use; all too often berthing manoeuvres go horribly wrong when the crew pulls the warps out of the locker and the helmsman has to wait while he untangles them.